Bunkie Life, Extra Space

Create a Beautiful Space for More Time
and Connection with Your Family

DAVID CAVAN FRASER

Dedication

To my wife Karrie and my three daughters, you're the reason that Bunkie Life exists. Also to my friends and family who supported us through the tough times.

CONTENTS

A Space to Connect

Some days, nothing happens.

You wake up, go through your routines, then go back to sleep. Like a loop. Other days, a moment rips you out of that loop and pulls you into an entirely new reality.

It was 2015. Life was good for me and my wife, Karrie. We'd not experienced major tragedy or disasters and had been blessed with a beautiful, healthy little girl, Evie, who was a year-and-a-half old.

We were a happy, loving family. And a growing family. That was important to us. We wanted a large family. I'd come from a large family myself and we loved the idea of having lots of kids around our home and also of having them all come visit us with families of their own as we got older.

With Evie's birth, we were well on our way to building the family we'd always dreamed of. But we had no idea of the heart-wrenching journey that lay ahead.

You may think this book is about building bunkies. After all, it's chock full of more than 250 high-resolution photos of beautiful bunkies in their natural Ontario habitat. The 12,000-plus words herein contain stories about happy bunkie owners and instructions for how to plan, design, build and beautify the perfect bunkie of your own.

However, if you think it's *just* about the bunkie, you've already missed the point. The *real* story of *Bunkie Life, Extra Space* is about meaningful connection – meaningful connection with family, friends, and with yourself. That's the essence of the Bunkie Life. The bunkie is just one vehicle to achieve it.

After reading this book, you *will* know the fastest, cheapest, and easiest way to get a beautiful, long-lasting, spacious bunkie at your home or cottage. And as you skim these pages, I hope you're thrilled by the photos and are captivated by the stories. However, my most *sincere* wish is that you're motivated to reflect on, and take action towards, meaningful connection with the important people in *your* life. If you do, you'll be well on your way to discovering the Bunkie Life in your own unique way.

PART 1

Meaningful Connection

Eighteen months after Evie was born, we learned that Karrie was pregnant again. We were elated. In the waiting room at the ultrasound clinic, I sparked up a conversation with another young dad-to-be.

"First one?" I asked.

"Yep", he replied.

"Oh, you're going to love it. Kids are the best", I told him, seizing the opportunity to be a parenthood evangelist, as always. "We've got one daughter now, but we want a *big* family."

I expected our "Dad banter" to be interrupted any moment by the ultrasound tech coming to get me so I could share the joy of seeing our thirteen-week-old baby for the first time in low-resolution, black and white beauty.

"Are you hoping for a boy this time?" he asked.

"Well, before Evie, I was like 'Son! Son! Son!' but she's so great. All I really care about is having a happy, healthy baby."

"Yeah for sure." He nodded in agreement.

2019 Bunkie with Loft overlooking the water on Birch Island.

Just then my wife came into the room, her face dark. "We've gotta go."

The doctor had told her that we'd lost the baby. We had come to the clinic to get our first, grainy glimpse of our little bundle of joy. Instead, our worst fears became a stark, painful reality.

As hard and unexpected as that news was, we soon learned it was a common experience, even if few people talked about it. These sorts of things happen, and Karrie and I agreed we would keep trying.

A few short months later, we were pregnant again. We lost the baby again. At the ten-week mark.

One miscarriage was a fluke. But two? So close together? We really started to worry that there was something more troubling at play ...

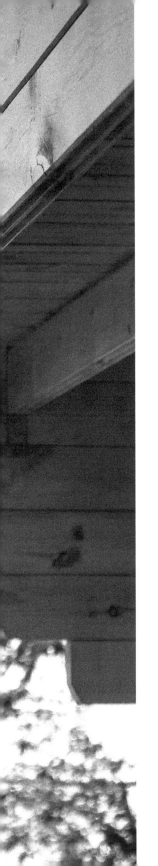

I

To Gather Together

What's great about Christmas morning?

Ask a small child, they'll probably say, "Presents."

Ask their parents and they'll probably tell you it's rediscovering the expectation, wonder, and joy of the season through their children's excitement.

But ask my mom, and I *know* what she'll tell you. She'll say, "It's having *everyone* back home ... *together.*"

At the phase of life my brothers and I are in, there's a lot going on: kids to raise, careers to build, businesses to run. Everyone lives in different parts of the globe, and the chances we have to gather all together are fleeting and rare.

2018 Bunkie with Loft alongside Bathroom Bunkie stained to match.

By the age of eighteen, we've already spent ninety-five percent of the time we'll ever spend with our parents. For the candy-inclined, if all the hours you'll ever spend with your kids were represented as a pack of Skittles, by the time they're eighteen years old, every Skittle would be gone but two.

That makes me feel nostalgic. It also makes me sad. But at the same time, it makes me realize how important it is to make the most of every opportunity we have to connect.

With the benefit of time, I now understand why my mom panicked the time I told her, "Mom, I don't think there's enough room for us at your place on Christmas Eve. We'll just get a hotel." That was *never* going to work. For Mom, everyone had to be back home, together, or it just wasn't Christmas.

Land O'Lakes

LESLIE H.
LAND O'LAKES, SOUTH EASTERN ONTARIO

My husband and I have five kids and eight grandkids. Three of our children and all our grandchildren live overseas, so we fly them home every summer for three weeks so we can all be together at the cottage. We often, at the same time, have my eighty-nine-year-old mother and her ninety-five-year-old partner with us too, as well as other extended family.

Sometimes we are twenty-five people strong for days at a time and we needed extra sleeping room, which it why we decided to buy our first bunkie.

I looked into several companies that sell bunkies, but the Bunkie Life website, and your story and enthusiasm, convinced me to contact you. You were such a joy to deal with, and the bunkie was so cute and so easily assembled. And when we had questions, you were always immediately available to help.

Given how many people we host at our cottage, it probably goes without saying that one bunkie was never going to be enough, and two years after building our first bunkie, we ordered and built our second one – a different model but just as cute.

Everyone who comes to the cottage loves them and so do we.

Thank you for making our bunkie experience a joy!

Our new bunkie will be a small painting studio. We may put in a fold-up bed for cottage overflow.

It sits amongst a series of perennial beds and backs onto a fast-flowing creek.

ANDREW P. AND GRAHAM M.
APSLEY, ONTARIO, NORTH KAWARTHA

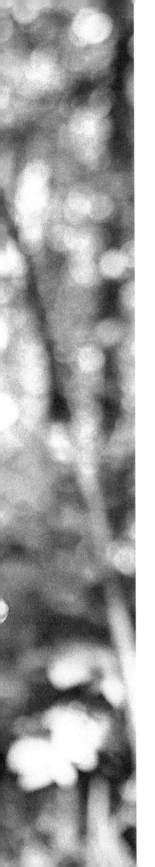

2

Where Does the Time Go?

5

Looking back over my calendar for last week, there's been a lot going on.

I met with twenty-five people to show bunkies at our home.

We hosted ten Airbnb guests at our property.

I had ten conversations with existing clients and twenty-five with potential clients.

I received four deliveries to our house.

Three people came by to provide quotes on various jobs we need completed.

I made five trips to the hardware store.

I painted the exterior of our house and stained a new bunkie.

I spent seven hours doing entrepreneurship training (an adult way of saying "homework"), twenty hours writing, and five hours filming and editing videos.

Phew!

Rustic 2018 Bunkie with Loft in the woods near Napanee River.   27

Karrie's calendar is even *more* packed with scheduling deliveries, answering e-mails, and homeschooling Evie, who's now in Grade 1. As busy as last week sounds, it's actually what we would call a "slow week"; often, it's much crazier. I consider it a win that we managed to have dinner together as a family every night except one.

I share this to illustrate the reality of modern life ... everyone is extremely busy. The pace of life feels so fast, and it seems to be speeding up, leaving little time to connect with one another. Hard data backs this up too:

- Canadians say they spend an average of almost eleven hours a day in front of various types of screens, according to a 2019 Leger Opinion survey.
- Seventy-six percent of Canadians say we're spending less time cooking and eating together as a family because we're too busy and more than two-thirds wish they could spend more time enjoying home cooked meals with their family, according to a 2019 survey commissioned by LG Canada.

In his song titled "Next Year" from the *Both Ways* album released in 2018, Donovan Woods laments how quickly time passes – how we make plans and "hope for the best". He astutely points out that despite our best intentions, we continually put off life's most important things until "next year", but sadly, "it's never quite next year".

Too often, we put off spending time with family, going on that trip, or reaching out to make that connection because there's so much we feel we have to get done *right now*.

Overwhelm and busyness affects everyone, and many great books have been written on the subject. Sidebar: I recommend *Getting Things Done* by David Allen or *The Power of Saying No* by Simon Wright if you're looking to go deep on the topic of time management.

But let's be honest. You're not likely to discover an empty calendar, and you'll rarely find the perfect time to spend the time or take the trip or make that connection – especially when it's not considered urgent. If you believe, like I do, that truly connecting with family is a vitally important value, then realize this: You don't *find* time and space for meaningful connection. You *create* it.

 BUNKIE LIFE STORIES

Tiny Township

WARREN H.

TINY TOWNSHIP
SIMCOE COUNTY, ONTARIO

We got our bunkie to use as an extra bedroom for our family cottage. My wife and I will use it as our bedroom and the kids will stay in the cottage with the grandparents. But we have put a mattress in the loft for the kids to sleep in also if they want to stay with us.

We're very proud of our bunkie.

We absolutely love our new bunkie! We use it for a little getaway on our "island". It is surrounded by marshland and lots of deer. We have been sleeping there almost every night since I finished it. I have also used it for extra sleeping space for the boys' weekend and when the in-laws were up.

We already live in a log home, but this allows us to use our entire property and even puts us deeper into the woods. Once I build the outdoor shower, rustic bathroom (aka outhouse), we will start promoting it on Airbnb as a rustic Whitetail Woods getaway. Eventually, I would like to buy more of them and put one on my second island.

MARK J.
CARLETON PLACE, ONTARIO

Found items on display near Stoney Lake, Ontario.   45

46

3

Where Are We Going to Put Everyone?

I'll confess that my wife and I struggle with "too much to do, not enough time to do it" mentality.

We're both first-born, go-getter, get-er-done-type people, and it's rare that we don't have multiple projects on the go every week.

When Evie was born, we converted our spare bedroom to a nursery. Karrie and I then realized that we quickly needed to figure out how to make space for visiting grandparents. Clearly, that comfy couch in the middle of the living room wouldn't cut it.

Always the proactive helper, my mom started sending me listings for tiny homes, glamping tents, and even yurts, which sent me down a "small-space rabbit hole" from which I didn't emerge for weeks!

Setting is everything for this wood-stove-equipped 2018
Bunkie with Loft near King City, Ontario.

Parkhill

STEPH & NICK I.

SYLVAN ALPACAS (SYLVANALPACAS.COM)
PARKHILL, ONTARIO

We got alpacas a few years ago as something to help eat the pasture and give our barn some use, and we soon started producing alpaca products (made from their fiber) and offering agri-tourism (alpaca walks). Alpaca fiber is comparable to cashmere but much stronger and more resilient and is considered one of the world's finest textiles.

57

Some of the products we produce from alpaca fiber are socks, insoles, yarn for knitting, and crocheted, stuffed alpacas.

We built our bunkie to use as a store in the summer. It's where we sell our alpaca products as well as some other locally made goods and it's just the right size (visually appealing too).

Stop by our farm and see us and walk with alpacas if you're ever in the Parkhill area! We love to teach people about these gentle, curious, and calm creatures.

Vintage display items add character to bunkie interior.

PART 2

Finding Space to Connect

In the wake of our two miscarriages, doctors couldn't really tell us what had caused them.

After we lost the first baby, the next pregnancy was monitored much more closely through constant bloodwork and more ultrasounds. Things got even more intense after the second loss.

In early 2016, we got pregnant once again (for the fourth time). Given the previous difficulties, we were subject to a whole slew of additional tests looking for immune disorders, blood disorders, and various deficiencies. Everything came back negative – in other words, no answers. Karrie was put on Progesterone and daily Aspirin with even more rigorous monitoring of bloodwork and ultrasounds as we spent the ensuing months oscillating between hope and anxiety.

Our fear, worry, and mourning turned to pure joy on October 19th when we welcomed our second daughter – appropriately named Hope – into our family.

Brightly coloured fabric and decorations create a lively interior.

The medications, treatments, and therapies had worked. The "issue" was solved. We were back on track with our dream of a big, child-filled family.

Little more than a year after Hope was born, we got more wonderful news. Karrie and I excitedly announced to Evie and Hope that there would be another little brother or sister joining our growing family. We were all jumping for joy, bouncing on the couch with excitement.

We could not have been happier or more grateful for the blessing we'd been given, especially after all the heartache we'd endured. It seemed those heartaches were over for good.

4

Expanding Space

After weeks of research into ways to expand our space to allow for regular visits from grandparents, I emerged, bleary-eyed, from my laptop. I'd compiled a list of every viable possibility that might help us host our parents while still keeping our little baby, Evie (we were getting pretty attached to her by then).

If you're looking to expand your space to allow for meaningful connection with your family or friends, you may consider some of the same options that I explored.

2018 Bunkie with Loft overlooking the Ottawa River.

Buy a Temporary Structure

The first idea I considered, based on the links my mom had sent, was putting up a temporary structure such as a simple tent, a more robust tent-like structure called a yurt, or a movable trailer. These proved to be relatively inexpensive, required no permits, could be erected quickly, and taken down or moved if need be. The main downside to tents is that they don't perform well in heavy rain, strong wind, or extreme temperatures. While trailers are more robust, Karrie and I weren't keen on adding a trailer-park aesthetic to our property.

Build an Addition

The next solution I considered was renovating our existing structure to add more space. The upside to this option is that the new, extended space is fully attached and integrated with your existing home or cottage. The downside is that renovations are a hassle, permits are needed, and renovations cost a lot in terms of money, time, and attention. As my mentor Mike Holmes often says, "Always budget two times what you think it will cost, and three times as much time with any renovation."

Move to a Bigger Place

A third alternative was to sell our place and buy a new, bigger one, hopefully in the same area and with all the features we needed. According to a realtor friend of mine who I consider to be a real expert, you should "expect to lose about six to eight percent of your property's value in various fees and commissions when you sell." That could translate to anywhere from $15,000 to $70,000 or more, depending on your situation. Of course, you'll also incur moving expenses and may have to pay more for the new place or sacrifice on the location or some of the amenities you already have. A lot of people have multiple generations of memories invested into their family home or cottage as well, which is something to consider. That was certainly the case with us and so we weren't at all keen to uproot our lives and move.

Build a Second Permanent Structure

Another option I considered was building a completely detached, secondary structure on our existing land. This felt like an appealing option at first, especially since some municipalities had recently updated regulations and introduced incentives for these types of projects to increase the stock of affordable housing.

A secondary structure typically has one or two bedrooms, a small kitchen, a living room, and a bathroom, and is fully insulated for all seasons. But on further investigation, I learned it would require a building permit and quite a large budget. A typical project starts around $120,000 but with an average cost of around $350,000, which was much more than we were prepared to spend.

The Perfect Solution?

I considered all these options for solving our space issue, but each one seemed to be lacking in some way. What if there was a way I could quickly and inexpensively create a beautiful space *without* a lot of time, hassle, or money? That's when I came across the perfect solution!

"I think we might need a bunkie", I told Karrie, confidently.

"What's a bunkie?" she replied, staring at me blankly.

"It's a little log cabin, separate from our house, for people to crash in. Best of all, it's small enough that we won't need a permit."

The 2019 Bunkie with Loft adds extra space on Round Lake.

What's a Bunkie?

A "bunkie", which is short for "bunkhouse", is a small cabin, often made of log, providing extra space for sleeping – about the size of a bedroom.

Where I live (in Ontario, Canada, which incidentally is where the term "bunkie" originated), most structures with a footprint less than ten meters squared (108 square feet) aren't considered a "building" by municipalities so no permit is required.

🌲 BUNKIE LIFE
FOOTPRINT

Most bunkie kits we sell in Ontario are under ten square meters, which, in most cases, eliminates the hassle of getting a building permit. In the United States, building codes vary, but most areas allow structures as large as 120 square feet without a building permit.

The more I looked into it, the more I was excited about the advantages of a bunkie, which it turned out are numerous:

- **Quick and easy to build.** Most people can construct a Bunkie Life kit over a weekend.
- **Hassle free.** Because of the size, a permit is not typically required, so you can just start building right away.
- **Relatively inexpensive.** A bunkie is quite economical, costing a fraction of what an addition or move would cost.
- **Attractive.** Bunkies can be built as a beautiful, attention-grabbing showpiece in your backyard or elsewhere on your property.
- **Durable and long-lasting.** Properly maintained, a bunkie can last for years.

More Than Just a Structure

But the real benefits of a bunkie go much deeper than practical ones. Perhaps the greatest benefit of a bunkie is the space it provides for meaningful human connection. Every day I hear stories from our clients about how their bunkie allowed them to bring their whole family together in ways they were never before able to do. They share the stories of how they bonded with friends, with their kids, and with their grandkids.

These moments of real connection with loved ones are so rare.

That's the essence of the Bunkie Life.

North Frontenac

ANONYMOUS

NORTH FRONTENAC TOWNSHIP
COUNTY OF FRONTENAC, ONTARIO

Our bunkie is great. We are using it for our family of four at our newly purchased land on a lake. We hope to build a full-sized cottage one day but will use our bunkie as a cottage until then, after which it will function as a guest cabin to host friends and family.

Here is a photo of our completed bunkie. We placed it on top of an existing deck about fifteen yards from our farmhouse and extended the deck to support the posts and create a larger sitting area from which to watch the sunset.

The bunkie is well designed, well thought out, and easy to assemble, particularly with all the videos available online.

We were looking for more accommodation space on our property. The entire extended family loves the bunkie, and the younger age group draw straws to see who gets to use it on any particular weekend.

GRANT M.
RED WING, ONTARIO (NEAR COLLINGWOOD)

We got a bunkie because we needed extra space for family visits. We put it on Airbnb because there is no place for people to stay in Petrolia. The cabin has a queen bed on the main floor with a double bed in the loft. It has a deck with a great view. Our property has lots of privacy and green space.

DEB F.
TREEHOUSE BUNKIE IN PETROLIA, ONTARIO

Gore's Landing

VIRGINIA & ERIC R.
GORE'S LANDING, ONTARIO

My 2019 bunkie with loft was a twenty-fifth wedding anniversary and sixty-fifth birthday gift (I chose it over a sparkly ring!).

I'd been looking around for a "she-shed" (including prefabricated garden sheds) for about five years but couldn't find anything I liked. My hubby, Eric, said if I designed what I wanted, he'd build it for me. It was a lovely

gesture, but it was never going to happen. Then, Bunkie Life popped up in my Facebook feed and the 2019 edition was perfect! Eric looked at it and said he couldn't build one for the cost of the kit (and the "two days to build" factor appealed to him).

A week before the bunkie kit arrived, Eric and his friend Derek spent five days marking out and laying the foundation. Then, when the kit arrived, they built the bunkie on the foundation as per the easy-to-follow instructions.

I had fun decorating the aptly named "Funkie Bunkie" with old and new things – handmade gifts from generous friends, a big moose canvas painted by my girlfriend, a sparkly chandelier floating from the roof beam on fishing line. Bright colours and many strings of mini lights, candles, and lanterns make it very magical at night. Eric says he's sure it can be seen from space.

Eric was offered early retirement in April so we like to wander up to the bunkie in the late afternoon and enjoy a drink together. I am hoping to be able to entertain my girlfriends there soon as well. It's a quiet, peaceful place to read a book or have an afternoon siesta.

I can't thank David (and Eric and Derek) enough for my little slice of heaven.

5

The Perfect Location

Once you've determined that a bunkie is the right solution for you and your needs, you have to determine where on your property you'll build it.

A flat level area with no trees is the easiest place to build. However, sometimes the most beautiful place to build is overlooking the water on a slope, or in the forest or up on the side of a hill. Each location has its own unique challenges to overcome, but the reward can be worth it for a great view.

Summer Cabin at Big Clear Lake, Ontario.

 BUNKIE LIFE STORIES

Larder Lake

DERECK & DEBBIE C.

LARDER LAKE
TIMISKAMING DISTRICT, NORTHEASTERN ONTARIO

We bought some property on Larder Lake in the Timiskaming District of Northeastern Ontario and decided to buy the 2019 Bunkie Life bunkie and a bathroom bunkie to put on the property. It is our summer getaway.

We first heard of Bunkie Life with the 2018 giveaway contest. We like the fact that we're supporting a small, family-run company.

The delivery driver was fantastic. We weren't there to take delivery and the road we're on isn't on any maps. And yet, the bunkie kit was perfectly placed in our driveway when we arrived!

We built a deck as a foundation to sit the bunkie on and the kit went together relatively easily. With just the two of us, we cleared the area, built the deck, assembled the bunkie, and stained it in two weeks. We then added the steel roof in August.

There is still some work to do inside and I will post progress when we get back next year.

P.S. Larder Lake was the site of the first gold rush in 1906 in Northeastern Ontario. It has a population of about 700 people, abundant wildlife such as moose and black bear, plentiful fish including lake trout, walleye (pickerel), and smallmouth bass, and endless boreal forests with hidden trails, streams, and rivers.

We're enjoying our bunkie in the sugar bush and waking up to deer. Fantastic product! We highly recommend to anyone looking for a kit bunkie. Gorgeous!

"RODNEY"
MCARTHURS MILLS, ONTARIO

The bunkie is pretty much finished. I had to wait until my daughter arrived yesterday to take a picture of me and my grandson in front of the bunkie. It was fun building with him (in spite of the heat, lately). The log pieces were good quality and fit together well. Your videos gave enough clues to the construction procedure, though no one explained what a "wind flap" was. We figured it out! It's now wired for lights, heat, and a fan, and my grandson slept out there for a few nights before leaving today. Everyone thinks it's a cute little structure.

LYNN H.

A Bathroom Bunkie is the perfect companion to a Bunkie Life bunkie.   119

6

Building Permits and Plans

While most areas don't require a building permit to build a bunkie, I still suggest you put in a quick call to your local township and ask them a few questions.

You can usually do this anonymously (without giving away your address or name) and I recommend recording the call (if it's legal to do so in your area) so that you have a record of what you're told.

Ask the following questions when you call the township:

1. **Size.** "I'd like to build a small structure that's under ten square meters. Do I need a building permit?"
2. **Height.** "Are there any height restrictions I should be aware of?"
3. **Location.** "What are the restrictions about where I can place the building (such as distance from a waterfront, from property line, or from other buildings)?"
4. **Anything else.** "Is there anything else I need to consider when building a small building on my property in this township?"

Be sure to get the person's full name and note the date of the call. Also be sure to save the call recording (or your notes) somewhere you can easily find it later, if needed.

Nestled in, overlooking the water at Jack Lake, Ontario.

Ask for Forgiveness Instead?

Could you just build your bunkie and not bother checking with your township? I don't recommend it. Why?

Most municipal issues are complaint driven. In other words, if your neighbours are cool, or far enough away to not care or even know about your bunkie, you might not have a problem. But even then, for peace of mind, it's worth making a quick call to the township to confirm that a permit isn't required (and to get the permit if it turns out it's needed).

Building Plans

Should you design your own plans, buy ready-made plans, or hire someone to design plans for you? There's no one right answer to the question. The good news is, if you're buying a bunkie kit, the plans will likely come along with it.

We send our Bunkie Life clients building plans via e-mail well ahead of their bunkie delivery so they can familiarize themselves with what needs to be done. You can also get these plans stamped by an engineer or with a Building Code Identification Number (BCIN), if required.

If you hire someone to design your plans, make sure they've got experience designing small buildings and have the recommended certifications. For example, in Ontario you don't need an architect, but hiring someone with at least a BCIN is recommended.

If you're buying ready-made plans, be sure they're compliant with local building code.

Designing your own plans is not for the novice and is best left to those with lots of carpentry or building experience.

2018 Bunkie with Loft, stained dark blue on Four Mile Lake in Ontario.   127

Kawartha Highlands

CHRIS AND LAURA

KAWARTHA HIGHLANDS, ONTARIO

After six months in Yemen working for the World Health Organization in 2017, I decided I needed to focus on myself and bought a piece of land in the Kawartha Highlands. We originally planned to build a cabin before realizing how difficult and expensive that would be.

We got a bunkie instead.

With the help of two friends, we built it over the Canada Day long weekend in 2018. The biggest effort was getting the twelve cinder blocks level. After that, it was clear sailing.

We've since built an outhouse, and installed a sink and shelves, and now that we have the bunkie, I really don't feel any need for a larger cabin.

We love it. We put it under the trees to keep it cool from the sun. It's the best thing I ever did.

We're planning to buy one more and rent it out on Airbnb so other people can enjoy the beauty of this area too.

Decor makes all the difference at this gorgeous Farlain Lake bunkie.   139

David stopped by Lake Rousseau to see the new bunkies at Muskoka Woods Resort, an overnight camp for kids ages six to sixteen years old. Muskoka Woods has the 2019 Bunkie with Loft, which they painted to fit in with all the other buildings on the site.

PART 3

Building a
Bunkie Life

When I built our first bunkie,
I thought I was just creating
a space for my parents and
in-laws to stay in when they
came to visit our family. That was
the motivation, but it turned out
to be so much more.

We'd soon find out that our bunkie wasn't just a place for hosting visitors. It was instrumental in getting our family through the most difficult situation we'd ever faced ...

Karrie and I and our two daughters were overjoyed about welcoming our third child to our family. Based on the success of our previous pregnancy, Karrie was put on the same Progesterone-and-Aspirin regimen and the constant monitoring was repeated. We knew the routine and were happy to comply since it had proven to be the "magic cure" we needed. Our girls started preparing too, talking about the new baby and putting aside some of their toys to give him or her as welcome gifts when the time came. On January 1, 2018, at the sixteen-week mark, the unthinkable happened.

No heartbeat.

The 2019 Summer Cabin provides a welcoming space for guests.   149

I was devastated. Karrie was devastated. We both struggled to find the words to tell everyone what had happened, especially our little girls who had been so excited.

We spoke to an army of doctors. Like before, there were no clear answers to why this was happening.

As sad as we were, though, we'd overcome this before and mustered the courage to try again.

Karrie became pregnant once more. Although what we thought had been a miracle cure had proven ineffective the last time, all the same measures were repeated. But again, around week seventeen, we lost our baby for the fourth time. The doctors ran genetic tests on me, Karrie, and the baby, and to everyone's surprise, everything came back "normal". We certainly didn't *feel* normal.

Neither of us knew how to cope. We had to continue being parents, keep running our business, and holding ourselves together emotionally. But all we wanted to do was give up. Life felt heavy. Colourless. I struggled to get out of bed every morning.

One day, a friend asked me some profound questions: "What do you think these babies would say to you if they could? What would they want you to do? Would they want you to give up? Would they want you to lie down in the grave *with* them?"

I knew in my soul that they wouldn't want that. They wouldn't want their death to claim any more people. I think they'd say, "Daddy, we can't feel the sunshine on our faces. We can't hold or comfort Mommy. We can't play with our sisters and tell them it's all going to be okay. But *you* can."

At that moment, I realized that I didn't have the choice to give up. I didn't have the luxury to numb myself. I needed to be there as best as I could as a husband. I needed to be there for the two daughters who needed me. It took me and Karrie a lot of time and many late-night conversations to realize that ultimately, being there for each other was the most important thing we could do. And I determined to look deep within myself to see how this situation could result in something good. It *had* to.

7

Your Bunkie– Building Team

With clearance from your township and building plans ready, there's one more thing you need to figure out before you're ready to build your bunkie. Who's going to do it?

About three-quarters of our customers purchase a Bunkie Life kit and then build it themselves (DIY). This is very feasible for most people because our kits are designed to be easy to build, even for someone inexperienced with construction.

However, if you're not at all handy, or simply don't have time to spend building over a weekend, you can hire a local contractor who you know and trust to build your bunkie for you. For our clients, we can also build their bunkie for them (for a fee) or recommend local contractors.

If you're like most and choose to build your bunkie yourself, I recommend asking some people to help. In fact, Bunkie Life kits require at least two people, but a team of three or more people is even better. It's a fun weekend project and the more people involved, the easier and quicker it is to complete.

The majestic 2020 Bunkie with Loft stands tall and feels spacious.

Scott Island

JACQUELINE M (AND FIVE FRIENDS)

SCOTT ISLAND, NEWBORO LAKE
RIDEAU CANAL, ONTARIO

Building this bunkie with five of my friends
— all women, aged fifty to seventy — was
cathartic and an amazing bonding experience.

In advance of the build weekend, we all
read the instructions, watched the videos,
and prepared. We started the foundation at
noon on Friday and quickly fell into a rhythm
and into roles that were comfortable for each
of us. On Monday, we put the last roof plank
on, and now have a sleeping bunkie on island
property on a lake with a beautiful view.

My advice for those wary of taking on a project like this is to be patient. Take time to read and re-read the instructions, review the videos, and take it step-by-step. Let the Bunkie Life team know when you are building it in case you get stuck and can't sort something out. They are an email away and very supportive.

My bunkie experience, from start to finish, was great – from placing the order, to the amazing delivery of the bunkie to Scott Island on a self-serve ferry barge, to me being a pain during set-up with my questions!

If we can build this thing, anybody can!

8

Bunkie– Building Tools

Before the build weekend, make sure you have all the tools you need to get the job done. The good news is that the requirements are pretty simple for every Bunkie Life kit.

Measuring Tape and Pencils

The logs in a Bunkie Life kit are pre-measured and pre-cut, but a measuring tape helps confirm the size and also helps for getting your bunkie square to start. If you're building from scratch, you'll have to measure each piece before cutting, so you'll use the measuring tape often. Bring pencils for marking distances as well.

Hammers

Hammers help for pounding logs into place. In addition to a standard-sized hammer, it's helpful to have heavier carpenters hammers and even a sledgehammer too.

This 2019 Bunkie with Loft provides the perfect escape for quiet contemplation.   171

Level

A level is another important tool to have on hand, and the longer it is, the better. You'll use the level to get your foundation ready for the structure and during the build to make sure everything is straight.

Cordless Drill

A drill will be useful in several places during the bunkie build, and a cordless one will be much more convenient, especially if your power supply is a distance away from your build site.

Small Air Compressor and Nail Gun

While you could use a standard hammer and nails to attach the floorboards and roof boards, if you have access to a small air compressor and a nail gun, the task will go a lot quicker.

Ladders

You'll need at least one ladder, but having a few on site (as many as four if you are able to borrow that many from neighbours, friends, or family) will be useful. Step ladders work great in most cases, but if you're building a bunkie with a loft, extension ladders (at least ten feet long) will be a big help.

Saws

If you're building a Bunkie Life kit, all the pieces are pre-cut to length so you shouldn't need a saw, but it's still not a bad idea to have one (either a hand saw or power saw) in case you need to cut a piece of trim or make an adjustment. If you're building from scratch, then you'll definitely need a power saw and possibly a mitre saw or two, since you'll be cutting each piece to size.

For more information on recommended tools, see bunkielife.com/tools.

South Frontenac

CHRISTINE L.
SOUTH FRONTENAC, ONTARIO

I had wanted a bunkie down in the woods at the bottom of my backyard for about ten years ... yes, ten years! My home backs onto the Napanee River. Having a place I could quietly escape to and listen to the trees was what I had in mind. I did my research and found Bunkie Life.

My boyfriend and I built the base for it a couple of weeks in advance so we would be ready when the kit arrived, and we managed to get that done without any arguing at all!

Then, my boyfriend and a couple of his buddies built the actual bunkie. They spent the day working hard, joking, and having lots of laughs. They started on a Friday and on the Saturday we put the roof and shingles on. It was a great opportunity to work together on a common goal.

It was also a great spending time together picking out the stain, and so relaxing watching the bunkie turn into my dream cabin.

My children are out on their own now, so when they visit, they love sleeping in the bunkie. It's like a getaway right at home! Friends and family have stayed in it, and I try to sleep in the bunkie a couple times a week too. Even just taking a book to read, and a handful of nuts to feed the chipmunks and squirrels is ideal. There's a special calmness being in the bunkie when it's raining, just lying in the loft looking out the window.

This 2019 Summer Cabin creates extra space for health and wellness.   183

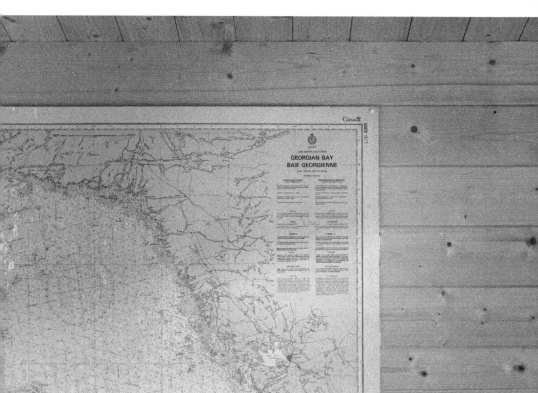

9

Let's Build

You've done all the prep work and have a team of helpers on site, ready to get to work.

It's time to build your bunkie, and there are just three phases to it.

Phase 1: Prepare your Area

Clear your build site of any trees that are directly in the build area. Most bunkies have a roof overhang, so your ten-by-ten-foot bunkie might actually be more like fifteen-by-twelve-feet.

If there are any branches overhead, trim them back before starting. It's annoying to be fighting off branches when you're trying to build your roof.

If your build site isn't perfectly level, you may need to add or remove soil. This can be a big job depending on how level (or un-level) your site is. Site prepping and laying the foundation (the next step) is usually about forty percent of the work in building a bunkie kit.

This 2018 Bunkie with Loft provides its owners much needed
extra space in the city.

Phase 2: Lay the Foundation

You have three options for your bunkie's foundation:

1. **Concrete pad.** Pouring a full concrete pad is expensive and more difficult than other options, but it should last a long time, if done properly.

2. **Concrete Pillars.** If you're in a frost-prone environment (like we are in Ontario), make sure you dig down below the frost line and then pour your concrete into tubes.

3. **Concrete blocks or patio stones.** This is the cheapest and easiest solution. Lay down lots of gravel before placing your blocks and then build up from there to get them level.

See bunkielife.com/foundation for more details about laying a solid foundation.

Phase 3: Build Your Kit

This is where the fun begins!

Make sure your first row of logs is level and square, then continue placing them on top of one another, row-by-row, pounding them down using a mallet or hammer. The windows and doors slide right into the pre-cut channels.

Bunkie Life clients often build our kits in one or two days with no prior experience, so if you finish earlier than planned, it will give everyone a chance to enjoy time together for the rest of the weekend.

One caution: Be sure to have lots of help when you're working on the roof. It's essential to have at least one person steadying the ladder and it's helpful to have a third person who can pass materials up to the person on the ladder.

Congrats! You're done!

For an example build, see bunkielife.com/buildin5minutes.

Almaguin Highlands

IAN & BELINDA

TORONTO, ONTARIO
BUNKIE IN ALMAGUIN HIGHLANDS, ONTARIO

Belinda is a budding metalsmith, making silver jewellery. We used to live in Oakville years ago and I converted a garden shed to a studio, but we sold the house and moved. For several years, Belinda had nowhere to work so the main purpose of our bunkie is for Belinda to use as a studio.

Building the bunkie was fun, exciting, and pretty straightforward. We had help as my parents were visiting from the UK and my father is an engineer. He took charge and project managed the build, first by checking

every single piece of wood and numbering it to match the plans! The actual build was much quicker than all of us thought and we all felt a great sense of accomplishment standing back and looking at what we'd built.

There is still a little work to do (building a deck around it, finishing the flooring, and outfitting the interior for Belinda's studio).

We are super delighted with the product.

🌲 BUNKIE LIFE STORIES

Trenton

MARK T.

TRENTON/BELLEVILLE, ONTARIO

We bought our bunkie because my son wanted to build a fort. I priced lumber and windows and was reluctant to go through with designing and building it. When we saw the Bunkie Giveaway, we entered and didn't win, but decided to buy one anyway to save me the work of designing and building a "fort."

The bunkie went together quite easy with some minor twists, and David was great answering any questions we had.

My son did the majority of the build (he

is only fourteen) and he's now living in the bunkie.

We have it wired up for electricity and put in three receptacles to run an air conditioner that I put in to keep it cool during the day and a small fridge for cool drinks and snacks. We bought some blinds for the front windows and door and a full-sized futon as well.

My son loves the bunkie. He has friends over and they spend most of the time in it.

P.S. We had about twenty centimetres of snow this week thanks to snow squalls off Lake Ontario. I thought the bunkie looked nice with the fresh snow on it. My son and I have slept out in the bunkie when it was around minus ten degrees Celsius. We had just a small electric heater that looks like a fireplace and the bunkie was toasty and warm all night.

The welcome mat says it all at this lovely 2019 Bunkie with Loft.   209

PART 4

Living the Bunkie Life

Sometimes when you're hurting, all you want is your mom. And with the emotional pain of our fourth miscarriage, Karrie and I needed our families more than ever.

We are so blessed to have loving, supportive parents. Although both sets of parents live far away, they were quick to drop everything and come to our sides.

Having a place where they could stay close by us while we were going through this time was so important. They could sit with us, cry with us, and just be there with us. That made all the difference.

Our bunkie became that place for us. A place where our parents could stay in our time of need. I'm not sure how we could have gotten through this most difficult time without their support and the space that made it possible.

We were healing.

After our sixth pregnancy (fourth miscarriage) our obstetrician referred us to the high-risk-pregnancy unit at Mount Sinai hospital in downtown Toronto. After a six-month wait, we finally met with the Mount Sinai team in January of 2019. They too were stumped for ideas but referred us to the genetics department for yet more tests.

Finishings can elevate the look of a bunkie, as with
this beautiful Buckshot Lake bunkie.

Again, everything came back "normal".

Ever since our last two miscarriages, Karrie had wondered why her platelet count was always high. This had been the case going as far back as our third and fourth pregnancies, but doctors had dismissed it, attributing it to one thing or another.

We pulled together the results of all her bloodwork over the years and Karrie realized that her platelet counts were virtually never in the normal range. She set about researching and came up with a hypothesis. Based on what she'd read, she thought there might be a chance that she had a mutation of what's called the "JAK2 gene". The JAK2 gene provides instructions for making a protein that promotes the growth and division of cells, and a mutation of this gene had been shown to be a significant risk factor for pregnancy complications. We contacted our genetics team at Mount Sinai and asked them about this long-shot theory, and they agreed to connect us with a hematologist to look into it.

That spring, we learned we were pregnant again and, as a result, we got in to see the hematologist quickly. After another battery of bloodwork, lo and behold, the one test that came back as abnormal showed that Karrie did, in fact, have the JAK2 mutation.

With a baby in utero, the clock was ticking. Karrie needed an immediate bone marrow biopsy and aspiration (removal of bone, fluid, and cells from the bone marrow) to get a proper diagnosis.

When the diagnosis came back, we were floored. Karrie had a rare cancer of the blood known as essential thrombocythemia in which your body produces too many blood platelets. Symptoms can include spontaneous blood clots in the arms and legs, which if left untreated could lead to heart attack and stroke. It also increases the risk of complications in pregnancy, which explained why we'd had so many miscarriages.

Through sleepless nights we wondered what the effects of Karrie's condition would be. Would she be able to live a full life? I couldn't even let myself consider a life without her and having to raise our two girls alone.

When we finally met again with the specialist, we learned that Karrie's condition was treatable and that she could expect to live a full, healthy life. And what's more? With the proper medication, there was no reason why we shouldn't be able to have more children. We finally exhaled.

She was put on a double dose of Aspirin and injections of a drug that would signal to her bone marrow to slow the production of platelets. For the rest of the pregnancy we would travel to Mount Sinai up to three times per week, every week.

Finally, on January 17th, 2020 we had our wonderful little miracle baby, Deklynn, in our arms.

Evie. Hope. Deklynn ... it had been a harrowing ride, but the growing family we'd always dreamed of was finally a reality.

Next-Level Options for Small Spaces

Over the years, I've found myself amazed at all the creative ways Bunkie Life clients customize their small spaces to create big connection. We could easily publish an entire book just featuring small space innovations (maybe we will — hint, hint!)

For the sake of time and space, I'll just give you a short list of ideas, but the possibilities are really endless.

Innovative Small-Space Heating Options

Our clients have turned us on to Montreal-based, Cubic Mini Woodstoves. They make tiny, fully functional wood stoves, complete with all the accessories needed to get your bunkie toasty-warm. We recently partnered with them and offer our clients a small discount on their products. Visit bunkielife.com/woodstove if you'd like to learn more.

If you're fortunate enough to have an electrical power source available to your bunkie, we've had great results with infrared heaters. Combine that with insulation (see below) and a heating blanket or mattress pad, and you'll find you or your guests can sleep cozy, even in chilly winter temperatures.

This 2019 Bunkie with Loft stands at the ready to host.   225

Insulation

A common question I get is, "Can I insulate my bunkie for all seasons?" Although our bunkie kits don't come with insulation, it's quite easy to insulate them for year-long use.

Most heat lost in a bunkie is through the roof and floor. For this reason, I recommend adding high density foam underneath the floor and above the deck boards, beneath the roof. Alternatively, you can use spray foam, which is more expensive, but insulates better.

To view some videos on this topic, visit bunkielife.com/insulation.

Stain

One of the most exciting times of the year is summer, when clients start sending photos of their bunkies, fully built, and finished with stain. When most people think of stain, they think of a generic brown colour, but that's just scratching the surface. Most wood stain can be tinted to almost any colour. Having tried a lot of products on the market, I have come to use, recommend, and love the stain from a Canadian company called Sansin Envirostain.

You can use thicker stains that cover up the wood or choose stains that allow the natural grain to show through. Plan to stain your bunkie within a year of building it to ensure it's protected from the elements so your family can enjoy it for many years to come.

I also recommend you spend a bit extra on a good quality stain. I've learned the hard way how difficult it is to remove the cheap stuff, and as I say for most things, "Do it right, do it once." Another benefit of a good quality stain is that you won't need to reapply it every year. Sansin stains only need a recoat every five years or so.

For more information about stains, visit bunkielife.com/stain.

Roof

While on the topic of "do it right, do it once",
let's talk about your bunkie roof. There are lots
of options to choose from: asphalt panels, slate
shingles, wood shakes, asphalt shingles, and
metal roofing.

Let's review them, one-by-one.

Asphalt Panels
Although they're the least expensive, I would
avoid asphalt panels if you plan to keep your
bunkie for longer than a few years, as they
don't hold up well and quickly start to look bad
and perform poorly.

Slate Shingles
A slate roof looks nice, but it's expensive, and
heavy, and will require an expert installer, so
it's typically overkill for a bunkie.

Wood Shakes
Wood shakes are absolutely beautiful, but the
cost is usually quite high, and shakes will eventually need to be replaced.

Asphalt Shingles
A standard shingle roof is reasonably inexpensive, and many clients choose this option, but
it takes a while to install and will eventually
need to be replaced.

Metal Roofing
If you can afford it, I suggest you spend a bit
extra and opt for a metal roof. It will last for-
ever, and as a wise man once said, "Do it right,
do it once."

A metal roof in the colour of your choice
should keep your bunkie investment protected
and looking great for many, many years.

A great company we recommend for metal
roofing is the Canadian company, Vicwest.

Power

Another common question I get is, "What about power to my bunkie?"

There are a few ways to wire up your bunkie. The best solution is to have an electrician come and properly wire a few outlets into the bunkie from the cottage or house. This will ensure you have lots of power and that it's installed correctly and safely.

Some customers go the DIY route and simply run an extension cord to the bunkie.

Make sure whatever you do complies with your local safety rules and building codes.

If running standard electrical power isn't an option, you can buy a small outdoor gas generator, but they can be smelly, loud, and a hassle to maintain.

A greener, quieter solution is a solar panel setup. Check out bunkielife.com/solar for more information on this option.

Bathroom facilities

A lot of would-be Bunkie Lifers wonder, "Where will my bunkie guests ... you know ... poop?"

That's a good question.

There are a few different options to choose from here also.

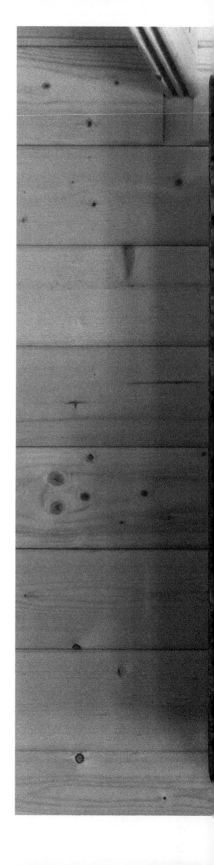

Bathroom Bunkie

At my place, Airbnb guests at my three bunkies all share one central "bathroom bunkie", which is just a dry wash basin and a composting toilet. Here in Ontario, any plumbing fixtures automatically require a building permit, so the self-contained, composting toilet we recommend and supply (the Sunmar GTG) is a good option that doesn't normally require a permit.

Some clients have installed gravity-fed shower barrels too. Having the bathroom as a separate structure allows you to have some private space separate from the bunkie and is a good solution in most scenarios.

For more information on this, visit bunkielife.com/bathroom.

All-in-One Bunkie and Bathroom

Another option is to build a bunkie that's big enough to have sleeping space *and* a separate bathroom. You *will* require a building permit for this, but if you don't mind the extra expense and time, this could be a great option.

In-House Bucket

One final alternative is the "in-house bucket", which involves installing a composting toilet (or makeshift sawdust bucket) right inside the bunkie for emergency situations, and guests then use the facilities in the main dwelling for "non-urgent" bathroom needs.

Union Jack Island

K. CLARKE

UNION JACK ISLAND
MUSKOKA, ONTARIO

I am so pleased with my bunkie and very proud of it! And our guests really enjoy it too!

The building process was more work than expected, because our ground wasn't level. The island has soft, forest floor so we had to dig holes and pour cement pylons.

The main body of the bunkie went up well but the roof was a lot of work because we chose shingles. Now I know why Dave recommends a steel roof – the pitch is steep so you

can't place the bundle of shingles on the roof, which makes them hard to install. But, for us, the shingles were worth the effort because it suits our cottage better.

We needed the extra space and our bunkie can sleep up to five. It truly is a sweet bunkie.

It's well built and I highly recommend it!

Kingston

D & S
KINGSTON, ONTARIO

Here are a few pics of our wonderful bunkie, which is named "Oh So Cool". There was a cottage with that name on the property in the fifties and sixties.

Everyone that comes to see it is blown away! We chose a Canadian theme, using Hudson's Bay fleece blankets and both new furniture and some antiques from our house. We chose twin beds so guests are more comfortable. You can see the layout from the pictures.

We absolutely love it! We have been having little parties out there with drinks and appies. The piece of land was unused before, and now it is so special. It gets sunrise and sunset – who knew!

All for now. Thanks again.

Renting
Out Your
Bunkie

Another cool option for your new bunkie is renting it out to earn extra income when you're not using it.

At our place in Ontario, we've been averaging about $10,000 in rent from each of our three bunkies. This extra $30,000 of income pays our entire mortgage and property taxes, which really helps steady the financial boat as things can get rocky as entrepreneurs sometimes.

There are a number of things to consider if you want to rent your bunkie out.

Do you have the space?

If you're using a bunkie in your backyard or at the cottage for you and your family and friends, that's one thing. It's a completely different thing if you've got rental guests coming and going. Is your bunkie relatively secluded from your living situation and your immediate neighbours? Will your neighbours have any issues with your bunkie hosting outside guests?

Quality doors and windows provide a touch of class to
this 2018 Bunkie with Loft.

Is your spouse on-board?

Most couples have a "gas person" and a "brakes person", since opposites attract. If you're the "gas person" when it comes to financial and investment decisions, it's a good idea to have a good, long conversation with your partner. Listen to their thoughts and objections and give them time to do research and thinking on their own. Karrie and I had multiple conversations before setting up our three Airbnb bunkies. We also started with just one.

Take a few moments with your partner to watch our Airbnb presentation at bunkielife.com/airbnb.

What about washrooms?

Washrooms are complicated since they often introduce the need for a building permit. One simple workaround is to just have a simple, outhouse-style bathroom and a self-contained, composting toilet. We have an agreement with a local gym that our guests can shower there on an inexpensive day pass. We've targeted very short-term vacationers, so most guests are fine with "roughing it" for a few days. You may go with a different setup, but there are multiple ways to solve this without it getting overly expensive.

Does your township allow short-term rentals?

Do your homework and research any restrictions in your area regarding short-term rentals, since not all municipalities allow them, and others have strict rules about what you can and cannot do.

How can you protect your investment?

Speak to your property insurance provider about what type of insurance you might need to protect your investment.

To minimize property damage, think about the stay from your guests' perspective. It's probably their first time experiencing your rental. I've found that creating a helpful "how-to" video for check-in and for all the amenities really helps your guests and results in fewer things being misused or broken due to a lack of understanding.

For an example of one of my how-to videos visit bunkielife.com/airbnbintro.

Kris and Jane were some of our first clients to take the plunge and do their own bunkie in Eastern Canada. They've had a great experience, hosting guests from all over the world and have paid for their bunkie many times over. They share the following three tips for renting out your bunkie:

- Post great photos of your property
- Price your listing competitively for the first while to get at least ten reviews
- Treat all your guests well, since word-of-mouth matters

If you'd like more detail on renting out your bunkie, my wife and I did two presentations on all the above topics. To learn more, visit bunkielife.com/airbnb.

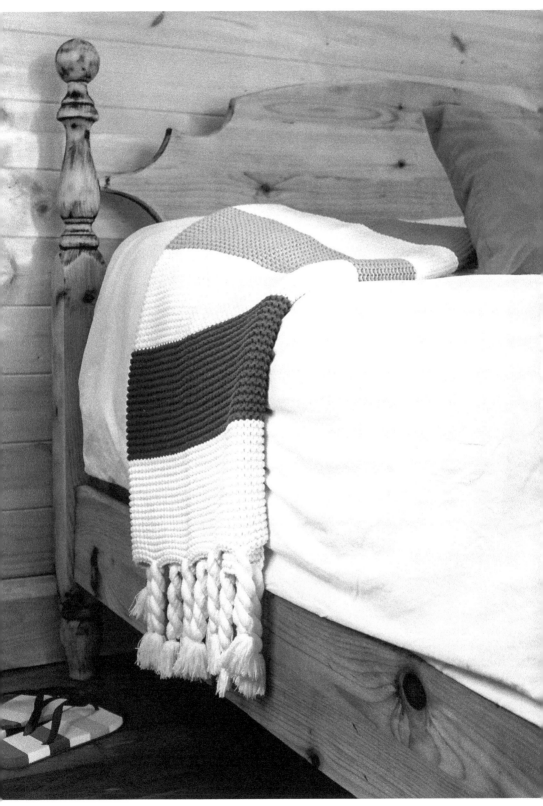

Stony Lake

CAROLYN S.

STONY LAKE
PETERBOROUGH, ONTARIO

I absolutely adore my new bunkie. I've pur-
posefully furnished it with vintage and found
items, such as my husband's grandmother's
chair, and a cot that I found curbside. I made
the decor from up-cycled linens and found
some of the decorative items (the glass and
pot on the shelf) on our lot.

Our bunkie is on our woodlot on the south
shore of Stony Lake, about half a kilometre
from the lake. We use the bunkie as a retreat

for me and my friends and we have aspira-
tions of renting it out on Airbnb or partnering
with charities to use it as a getaway for ladies
who need a respite from their obligations,
whatever those may be.

257

Dogwood Lake

HEATHER & KYLE

DOGWOOD LAKE
EASTERN ONTARIO

Check out this bunkie beauty on Dogwood
Lake in Eastern Ontario – twenty minutes
north of Kingston and twenty-five minutes
Southeast of the Thousand Islands. Open
your door to the beautiful lake, go for a swim,
a lovely canoe ride, or toast some marshmal-
lows around a campfire at night.

    "The bunkie was the absolute perfect addi-
tion to our property. If there was more room,
we would love to have another one."

The stunning floors are Shou Sugi Ban (or Yakisugi), which is an ancient Japanese technique of preserving and finishing wood using fire. Owners, Heather and Kyle, used a hand torch to char the wood themselves and it turned out beautifully.

You can rent Heather & Kyle's Airbnb bunkie and cottage by visiting the link at bunkielife.com/airbnb.

Lake Manitou

MARTIN P.

LAKE MANITOU
MANITOULIN ISLAND, ONTARIO

We decided to build a bunkie to add some sleeping space at our cottage for my stepson and his friends as well as other guests.

The build was like building an Ikea product (more complicated, but the instructions are similar) and it all went together very well. It's a quality product.

Although it took three weeks to build, I basically built the whole thing myself, including laying the foundation, assembling the

structure, and installing the steel roof and the deck on the front (with a little help). I also stained the floor to give it a little contrast inside. Even the large beams that run across the roofline I did myself. With a couple of extra hands, I suspect the build would have taken only about three or four days. Plus, I consider myself only moderately handy, so there was a bit of thinking time that had to take place (I had never done a steel roof before, so I had to figure that all out, for example).

I am very happy with the finished bunkie and would be happy to be a reference for the product.

Your Bunkie Life?

While I was in the hospital with Karrie and Deklynn, I met a fellow dad who had just spent sixty days with his wife and premature baby at Ronald McDonald House. They were fortunate enough to be able to stay there through that period and it made their situation easier to manage. Another friend of mine found out just days before his daughter's birth that she'd need emergency surgery and an extended stay at SickKids Hospital. They too were able to stay at Ronald McDonald House so they could be close to their daughter in her time of need.

Having family there when you need them is so important – it certainly has been for us these past few years. We've been so blessed, and as Karrie and I were looking for ways that our situation could help others, we realized something. We had built our own little Ronald McDonald House right in our backyard and we didn't even know it. The bunkie had allowed our family to be close to us and support us while we were hurting, just like Ronald McDonald Houses do for so many families. It was then that we committed that for each Bunkie Life kit we sold, we'd donate the cost of a night's stay in a Ronald McDonald House for a family in need. All proceeds from this book will go to Ronald McDonald House charities as well.

For our family, Bunkie Life is more than a business. It's a way of life and a way we can help create good in the world.

It's kind of funny the way it turned out. It all started as a simple solution to the simple question, "Where are we going to put everyone?"

Maybe you're asking a similar question. Maybe a bunkie might be the solution *you* need to create meaningful connection.

Modern life is busy. It can block our attempts at quality time with people we love. I shared my story about how our bunkie created the space for our family to regroup and connect during a tragedy. You've learned about the different options I considered and why I ultimately chose a bunkie as the fastest, easiest, and most cost-effective way to add the extra space we needed. You also learned how to build your own bunkie, so it's done right, and done once, and also learned a few ways you can take your bunkie to the next level.

So now it's time to act. It's time to make space for the connections that are important in your life.

Don't wait for the perfect time or for complete knowledge. Some people spend years looking at photos of cabins and bunkies, fantasizing about where it will go and how they'll decorate it. They imagine the freedom and memories their perfect bunkie will create for them and their loved ones. Unfortunately, for a lot of people, that's where it ends: dreaming.

Why?

Because they never take any action towards turning those dreams into reality. I often wonder why that is and have concluded that it comes down to two things:

1. **Knowledge.** You've read this book, have seen what's possible and know how the bunkie has changed my life and the lives of our clients. You may be ready now, or there may be more research needed for your specific situation. You're always welcome to reach out to me personally at david@bunkielife.com if there's anything I can help with.

2. **Belief.** Until you truly *believe* that space for meaningful connection with your family and friends is essential, you'll never experience the full depth of human relationship that's possible in your life. If you say you believe that family comes first, but never learn about ways to better connect and never create the space to spend time connecting, can you really claim that you truly *live* that principle? Ultimately, we prove what we really believe by what we focus on and by what we actually *do*.

"You don't have to be great to start, but you have to start to be great."

– Zig Ziglar

When I started my bunkie life journey, I hadn't built much of anything. I hadn't taken shop class, and had spent most of my adult life with my hands on guitar strings, not power tools. I still don't consider myself a skilled carpenter, but I found a kit solution that worked for my limited skillset and I took action. If I'd waited until I was an expert to start my bunkie, I would never have started. We'd never have started our own successful Airbnbs, we'd have never started selling our kits to others, and I'd have never written this book.

If there's one thing I hope you take away from this book it's this: take action and *do* something to connect with people. A small, imperfect step with limited knowledge is far better than a perfectly informed step that you never actually take. A wise man once said: "You don't need to know the entire journey, just the next few steps."

If you're thinking of building a place for meaningful connection in your life, I'd love to invite you to reach out to us and see how we might be able to help. Visit www.bunkielife.com or call us directly at 1-866-4BUNKIE and we can help you take your first step to meaningful connection.

If, after reading this book, you're not yet sure if a bunkie is the right solution for you and your loved ones, I'd like to invite you to take our 3 minute "Are You Ready For the Bunkie Life?" quiz by visiting bunkielife.com/quiz.

About David Fraser

David Fraser and his wife Karrie purchased their first bunkie in 2015 so they could have space for their parents to stay overnight when visiting the grandchildren.

Their house wasn't large enough for everyone, and David's mom was tired of sleeping on the couch, so she encouraged them to build something on their property, and so he set about searching for a solution. He wanted to find something that was relatively easy to build at a reasonable price. He also didn't want the hassle of needing to get a building permit.

That's when David discovered bunkies – ones you can build from a kit.

They ordered a bunkie kit and David and his dad built their bunkie in one weekend. David and his family loved it so much that he began designing and selling his own kits that can be assembled quickly, easily, and inexpensively.

David and Karrie now have three more bunkies on their property that they rent out on Airbnb as getaways from the city and they're booked almost every night, year-round.

David and his team know what features are important in a bunkie and offer cabin bunkie kits, custom bunkies, and a variety of quality, reasonably priced add-on options to take your bunkie to the next level.

Reach out now to discover the Bunkie Life of your own.

www.bunkielife.com
david@bunkielife.com
+1 (866) 4BUNKIE

About Bunkie Life

At Bunkie Life, we make it easy to build a safe, comfortable and great looking cabin without a second mortgage or a building permit.

We're experts in creating space for human connection
Bunkie Life is a Canadian company specializing in small log cabin kits that can be easily built in a weekend without a permit. We're helping hundreds of clients all over Ontario and other parts of Canada.

Bunkie living has never been so big
Our social media presence has gone viral, attracting tens of thousands of followers across YouTube, Instagram, and Facebook, as well as our private email list of over 100,000 current and prospective clients who are excited to be part of the Bunkie Life community.

Featured on HGTV
One of our bunkies was featured on a new HGTV show, *Family Home Overhaul*, which debuted in the fall of 2020.

More than just a bunkie kit
At Bunkie Life, we don't just provide a high-quality cabin at a great price. We stand behind our products to make sure that everybody is a super pumped up promoter of what we do and what we stand for.

www.bunkielife.com
david@bunkielife.com
+1 (866) 4BUNKIE

 fb.com/bunkielife
 @bunkielife

Published by Grammar Factory Publishing, an imprint of MacMillan Company Limited.

Grammar Factory Publishing
MacMillan Company Limited
25 Telegram Mews, 39th Floor, Suite 3906
Toronto, Ontario, Canada
M5V 3Z1
www.grammarfactory.com

Fraser, David C.
    Bunkie Life, Extra Space: Create a Beautiful Space for More Time and Connection with Your Family / David C. Fraser.

Hardcover ISBN 978-1-989737-22-4
eBook ISBN 978-1-989737-23-1

1. HOM023000 House & Home / Small Spaces. 2. HOM013000 House & Home / Outdoor & Recreational Areas. 3. HOM005000 House & Home / Do-It-Yourself / General.

Production Credits
Printed in Canada
Design by Dania Zafar
Book production and editorial services by Grammar Factory Publishing

CPSIA information can be obtained
at www.ICGtesting.com
Printed in the USA
BVHW050444230322
632129BV00001B/2